COUNTRY PROFILES

DENMARK

BY CHRISTINA LEAF

BELLWETHER MEDIA • MINNEAPOLIS, MN

Blastoff! Discovery launches
a new mission: reading to learn.
Filled with facts and features, each
book offers you an exciting new
world to explore!

This edition first published in 2020 by Bellwether Media, Inc.

No part of this publication may be reproduced in whole or in part
without written permission of the publisher.
For information regarding permission, write to Bellwether Media, Inc.,
Attention: Permissions Department,
6012 Blue Circle Drive, Minnetonka, MN 55343.

Library of Congress Cataloging-in-Publication Data

Names: Leaf, Christina, author.
Title: Denmark / by Christina Leaf.
Description: Minneapolis, MN : Bellwether Media, Inc., 2020. |
    Series: Blastoff! Discovery: Country Profiles | Includes bibliographical
    references and index.
Identifiers: LCCN 2019001496 (print) | LCCN 2019002725 (ebook)
    | ISBN 9781618915894 (ebook) | ISBN 9781644870488
    (hardcover : alk. paper)
Subjects: LCSH: Denmark–Juvenile literature.
Classification: LCC DL109 (ebook) | LCC DL109 .L43 2020 (print)
    | DDC 948.9–dc23
LC record available at https://lccn.loc.gov/2019001496

Editor: Rebecca Sabelko   Designer: Brittany McIntosh

Printed in the United States of America, North Mankato, MN.

TABLE OF CONTENTS

SKAGEN

A family heads to Skagen, the city at the northernmost tip of Denmark. Outside of town, the family sees how sand affects the area. First, they pass the Råbjerg Mile. This dune moves across the land each year, pushed by wind. Just beyond the dune, a church tower sticks out of the ground. It was abandoned after sand drifts grew too high.

OTHER TOP SITES

BORNHOLM

KRONBORG CASTLE

LEGOLAND

TIVOLI

Art museums are scattered throughout the small town. Artists have long been inspired by the area's natural beauty. In the afternoon, the family heads to the beach. At Denmark's northernmost point, the waves of two seas crash together in a spectacular show. This is Denmark!

MORE DENMARK

The Kingdom of Denmark includes two territories. Greenland, the world's largest island, is in the Atlantic Ocean. The Faroe Islands are also in the Atlantic, north of Scotland.

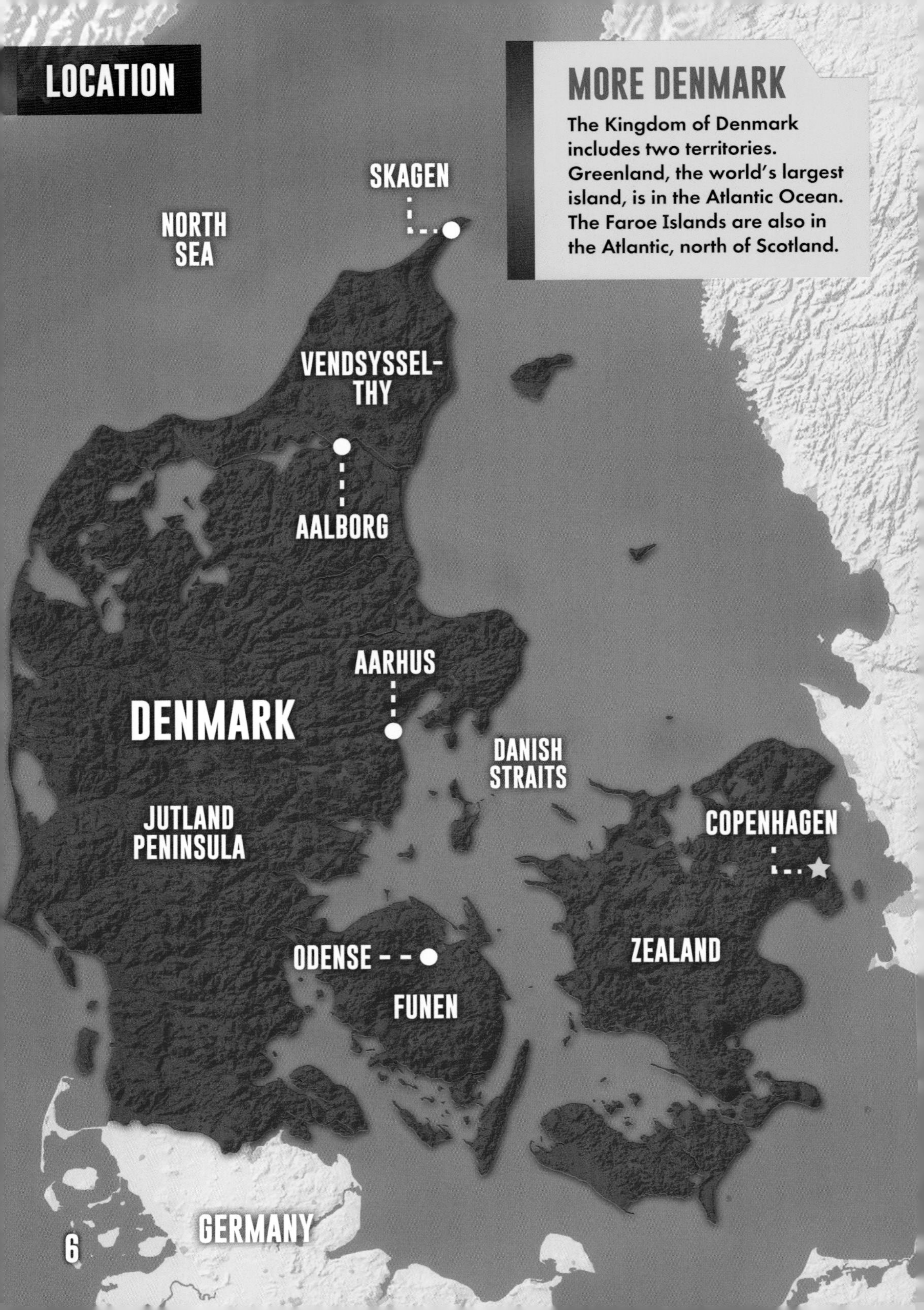

SKAGEN

NORTH SEA

VENDSYSSEL-THY

AALBORG

AARHUS

DENMARK

DANISH STRAITS

COPENHAGEN

JUTLAND PENINSULA

ZEALAND

ODENSE

FUNEN

GERMANY

Denmark covers 16,639 square miles (43,094 square kilometers) in the north of Europe. With Sweden and Norway, it makes up a region called **Scandinavia**. Denmark's land consists of the Jutland **Peninsula** and many islands. The largest islands are Funen, Vendsyssel-Thy, and Zealand. Denmark's capital, Copenhagen, is on the far east side of Zealand.

Denmark's only neighbor by land is Germany to the south. The North Sea borders Denmark to the west and north. To the east, most of Denmark's islands rest in the Danish **Straits**. The Straits connect the North Sea to the Baltic Sea.

BALTIC SEA

LANDSCAPE AND CLIMATE

Long ago, **glaciers** shaped much of Denmark's land. They left eastern Jutland mostly flat with low, rolling hills. The jagged eastern coast holds many small **inlets**. The Lim **Fjord** separates the rich **plains** of Northern Jutland from the rest of the peninsula. Sandy beaches line Jutland's western coast, with **marshes** soaking up salty seawater in the southwest.

THY NATIONAL PARK
VENDSYSSEL-THY

BORNHOLM

COPENHAGEN

Average seasonal highs and lows

JANUARY
HIGH: 36 °F (2 °C)
LOW: 28 °F (-2 °C)

APRIL
HIGH: 50 °F (10 °C)
LOW: 36 °F (2 °C)

JULY
HIGH: 68 °F (20 °C)
LOW: 55 °F (13 °C)

OCTOBER
HIGH: 54 °F (12 °C)
LOW: 45 °F (7 °C)

°F = degrees Fahrenheit
°C = degrees Celsius

Most of Denmark's islands match the rolling landscape of eastern Jutland. Far away in the Baltic Sea, the island of Bornholm is rocky with tall cliffs.

The ocean controls much of Denmark's weather, leaving a **temperate** climate. Winters are cold with snow, but summers are mild.

OTTER

Denmark is home to many types of birds. Red kites, harriers, and other raptors swoop through the skies, hunting small mammals like hares and voles. Common kingfishers and wading birds such as storks scan waters for fish, frogs, and insects. **Migrating** starlings gather in such large groups that they block the sun when they take off.

LION'S MANE JELLYFISH

Recently, wolves have reappeared in Danish lands. They hunt for roe deer and red deer wandering Jutland's forests and fields. Otters play in the peninsula's rivers and lakes. Seals and whales such as humpbacks swim in the seas around Denmark. Several kinds of jellyfish float off its shores.

RED KITE

A NOT-SO-UGLY ANIMAL

Denmark's national animal is the mute swan. This bird famously stars in *The Ugly Duckling*, written by Denmark's famed storyteller, Hans Christian Andersen.

RED DEER

RED DEER

Life Span: up to 18 years
Red List Status: least concern

red deer range =

LEAST CONCERN	NEAR THREATENED	VULNERABLE	ENDANGERED	CRITICALLY ENDANGERED	EXTINCT IN THE WILD	EXTINCT

Almost all Danes have Danish backgrounds. But small German populations live along the Germany border. **Immigration** has brought people from Turkey, Eastern Europe, Africa, and the **Middle East**.

Most people in the country speak Danish, the official language. English is a common second language, but immigrant populations speak other languages, too. Lutheranism is the country's official religion, but people are free to practice whatever they wish. Islam has grown in recent years. Many Danes do not follow any religion.

FAMOUS FACE

Name: René Redzepi
Birthday: December 16, 1977
Hometown: Copenhagen, Denmark
Famous for: Founder and head chef at Noma, which has been ranked the number one restaurant in the world four times

SPEAK DANISH

ENGLISH	DANISH	HOW TO SAY IT
hello	hej	hi
goodbye	farvel	fah-VEL
please	vær så venlig	var saw VEN-lee
thank you	tak	tahck
yes	ja	yah
no	nej	nai

COPENHAGEN

Most Danes live in big cities such as Copenhagen or Aarhus. They may live in apartments or single-family houses. Newer Danish houses tend to be **energy-efficient** and feature modern designs. Families are small, and many Danes live on their own or wait to start families. Houses in the country are often on small farms.

Danish people have many ways to get around. Trains cross the country, and cars and buses help people get around in cities. Bicycles are extremely popular, and bicycle lanes zigzag through cities.

At the center of the Danish lifestyle is *hygge*. This word refers to relaxation and appreciating smaller joys in life. People gather with old friends for good conversation. They also find coziness at home with candles or a roaring fire.

HAPPIEST PLACE ON EARTH

Denmark has often been ranked as the happiest country in the world. Danes enjoy a high level of social equality and a good standard of living.

Sustainable living is very important to Danes. Their reduced chemical use on farms has helped them become world leaders in producing **organic** foods. In their daily lives, Danes cut down on energy use at home and use public transportation or bicycles to get around. Much of the energy they do use is from **renewable** sources like wind.

Children in Denmark attend school between ages 6 and 16 as well as one year of preschool. Students learn in Danish, but they also learn English early on. Schools encourage active learning and participation. Over half of Danish students go on to higher education. Denmark also emphasizes life-long learning, so people may attend school for work or pleasure.

Most Danes have **service jobs** or work in **manufacturing**. Those in services most often work in education or health. Manufacturers make food, shoes, wood products, and machinery. Denmark also makes most of the world's windmills. Farms cover much of Denmark. Grains, dairy, and pork are common products.

MAKING CANDY

LEGOLAND

Billund, Denmark is home to the world headquarters of the LEGO Group. It is one of the most popular toy brands in the world!

TIVOLI

In Copenhagen, people may go to Tivoli for a bit of fun. This amusement park sits in the heart of the city. It offers rides, restaurants, ballet, concerts, and much more!

Danes love to spend time outdoors. They explore the natural areas of their country by hiking and bicycling. Many enjoy spending time on the water by kayaking, sailing, or swimming. Even Copenhagen has a few natural swimming areas in the harbor. Danes may also bring nature to their homes with gardens.

SAILING

Danes have won Olympic medals in many sports including canoeing and rowing, but soccer is their favorite sport. Tennis, handball, and swimming are also popular. When winter comes, Danes may get outside on ice skates or cross-country skis.

SOCCER

MUS (MOUSE)

Mus is a game commonly played at Christmastime, but you can play it any time of the year!

What You Need:
- a few handfuls of nuts, pennies, or similar items

How to Play:
1. Place the items in the middle of all the players. The group chooses one person to be the catcher. The catcher closes their eyes, and the rest of the players choose one item to be the mouse.

2. When the catcher opens their eyes, they must take items one by one from the middle without choosing the mouse. If they take the mouse, the other players yell "Mouse!" Then that player counts how many items they took before putting them back in the middle.

3. Then the next player takes a turn with a new mouse. The game is finished when everyone has taken a turn. The player who took the most items wins!

FISH MARKET

Sustainable, local ingredients are gaining popularity in Danish cooking. Fish such as herring, cod, or salmon is common in meals. Pork and root vegetables also appear frequently. Denmark's national dish, crispy pork with parsley sauce and boiled potatoes, is a favorite meal that dates back centuries. Salty black licorice is a popular treat.

Breakfast is usually light. Danes may have cereal with milk or a pastry. For lunch, Danes often eat *smørrebrød*. These open-faced rye sandwiches are topped with fish, eggs, cold meat, or potatoes. Families often gather for dinner and eat a bigger meal.

CRISPY PORK DISH

SMØRREBRØD

RØDGRØD MED FLØDE

Ingredients:
2 cups red berries or fruit
   (strawberries, red currents, raspberries,
   rhubarb, blackberries)
1 cup water
1/2 cup sugar
1 tablespoon cornstarch
whipped cream or half and half

Steps:
1. Combine fruit, sugar, and water into a large pot. With an adult, bring to a boil, then simmer for 2 to 3 minutes.

2. Strain the fruit mixture through a strainer or cheesecloth. Then add the cornstarch and cook over medium heat until it thickens, about 8 to 10 minutes.

3. Pour the mixture into individual bowls and chill for at least 2 hours.

4. Serve with half and half or whipped cream!

TASTY TONGUE TWISTER

The popular *rødgrød med fløde*, or red berry pudding, has many unique Danish sounds in its name. Danes love hearing foreigners try to pronounce it!

CELEBRATIONS

Many Danish celebrations follow the Christian calendar. Before Lent, in February or March, Danish children celebrate *Fastelavn*. They dress in costumes and play cat-in-a-barrel, a piñata-style game. On Easter, kids send unsigned letters. If they stump the receiver, they win a chocolate egg!

Christmastime in Denmark is filled with festivities! In the 24 days leading up to Christmas Day, children enjoy Advent calendars. Many calendars offer a small present each day. The Danes decorate their homes with trees, fir branches, and lights. On Christmas Eve, families gather for a meal and often dance and sing around the Christmas tree. Holidays are one way Danes find joy in life!

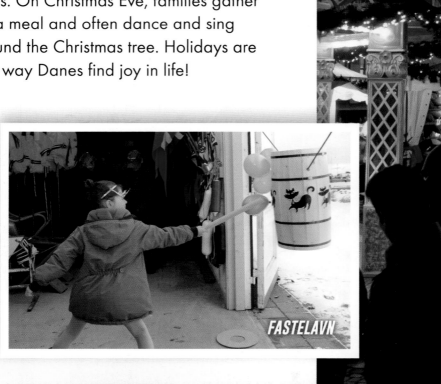

FASTELAVN

JUST ANOTHER DAY

Denmark does not have an official national holiday. Constitution Day on June 5 is the closest, but big celebrations are uncommon. Most people spend the day with their families, since it is also Father's Day.

THE WHITE CHRIST

CHRISTMAS MARKET

TIMELINE

AROUND 793
The Viking Age begins as ancient Scandinavians attack an English island

1849
Denmark's first constitution is signed

900s
Denmark unifies under King Harald Bluetooth

1729
Greenland becomes part of the Kingdom of Denmark

1397–1523
Denmark, Sweden, and Norway become one country called the Kalmar Union

1940
Germany occupies
Denmark during
World War II

2011
Helle Thorning-Schmidt
becomes Denmark's first
female prime minister

1972
Queen Margrethe II
is crowned

2005
Cartoons in a Danish
newspaper showing
the Muslim prophet
Muhammad spark
worldwide protests
among Muslims

DENMARK FACTS

Official Name: Kingdom of Denmark

Flag of Denmark: Denmark's flag is a red rectangle with a white cross. The short arm of the cross is slightly to the left of the center. This cross is known as the Nordic cross, and Denmark shares it with the rest of the Nordic countries. Denmark has one of the oldest national flags in the world, adopted in 1219.

Area: 16,639 square miles
(43,094 square kilometers)

Capital City: Copenhagen

Important Cities: Aarhus, Odense, Aalborg

Population:
5,809,502 (July 2018)

WHERE PEOPLE LIVE

COUNTRYSIDE
12.1%

CITY
87.9%

MANUFACTURING
18.3%

JOBS

FARMING
2.4%

SERVICES
79.3%

Main Exports:

machinery   furniture   meat

medicine   wind turbines

National Holiday:
Constitution Day, June 5

Main Language:
Danish

Form of Government:
parliamentary constitutional monarchy

Title for Country Leaders:
queen (head of state), prime minister (head of government)

RELIGION

EVANGELICAL
LUTHERAN
74.8%

OTHER
19.9%

MUSLIM
5.3%

Unit of Money:
Danish krone

GLOSSARY

energy-efficient—uses little energy to function

fjord—a narrow part of the ocean between cliffs or steep hills or mountains

glaciers—massive sheets of ice that cover large areas of land

immigration—the act of moving from one country to another

inlets—narrow bays in the shore of a body of water

manufacturing—a field of work in which people use machines to make products

marshes—wetlands that are filled with grasses

Middle East—a region of southwestern Asia and northern Africa; this region includes Egypt, Lebanon, Iran, Iraq, Israel, Saudi Arabia, Syria, and other nearby countries.

migrating—traveling from one place to another, often with the seasons

organic—produced without the use of chemicals

peninsula—a section of land that extends out from a larger piece of land and is almost completely surrounded by water

plains—large areas of flat land

renewable—able to be replaced

Scandinavia—a region of northern Europe that includes Sweden, Denmark, and Norway

service jobs—jobs that perform tasks for people or businesses

straits—narrow channels connecting two large bodies of water

sustainable—able to be used without being completely used up or destroyed

temperate—associated with a mild climate that does not have extreme heat or cold

TO LEARN MORE

AT THE LIBRARY

Gifford, Clive. *Denmark*. London, UK: Wayland, 2015.

Klantan, Robert, and Hendrik Hellige, eds. *Andersen: The Illustrated Fairy Tales of Hans Christian Andersen*. Berlin, Germany: Gestalten, 2017.

Murray, Julie. *Denmark*. Minneapolis, Minn.: Abdo Publishing, 2018.

ON THE WEB

FACTSURFER

Factsurfer.com gives you a safe, fun way to find more information.

1. Go to www.factsurfer.com.

2. Enter "Denmark" into the search box and click 🔍.

3. Select your book cover to see a list of related web sites.

INDEX

The images in this book are reproduced through the courtesy of: giannimarchetti, cover;
Walter Bibikow/ Getty, pp. 4-5; janmadsen, p. 5 (top); Andrey Shcherbukhin, p. 5 (top middle);
RPBaiao, p. 5 (middle bottom); Anastasia Pelikh, p. 5 (bottom); AridOcean, pp. 6-7, 8; Traveller70,
p. 8; Mariusz Switulski, p. 9; mikecphoto, p. 9 (right); Rafal Szozda, p. 10 (left); Popova Valeriya,
p. 10 (top); Martin Prochazkacz, p. 10 (middle); Huy Thoai, p. 10 (bottom); Paolo-manzi,
pp. 10-11; Arctic Images/ Alamy, p. 12; DavidCC/ Alamy, p. 13 (top); Devteev, p. 13 (bottom);
Milosz Maslanka, p. 14; Realimage/ Alamy, p. 15; Marija Vujosevic, p. 16; Dan Bach Kristensen,
p. 17; View Pictures/ Getty, p. 18; Dirk Renckhoff/ Alamy, p. 19 (top); lemon stocks, p. 19;
Niels Quist/ Alamy, pp. 20 (top), 24 (left), 24-25; Brijo, p. 20; mooinblack, p. 21 (top); CapturePB,
p. 21; Radiokafka, p. 22; EsHanPhot, p. 23 (top); Artmim, p. 23 (middle); JanMacuch, p. 23
(bottom); Valentinian/ Wiki Commons, p. 26; Slavko Sereda, p. 27 (top); Pacific Press/ Alamy, p. 27;
Ivsanmas, p. 28; Necessary E/ Wiki Commons, p. 29; a-ts/ Alamy, p. 29 (right).